Native Americans

Subarctic Indians

Mir Tamim Ansary

Heinemann Library
Chicago, Illinois

Customer Service 888-454-2279

Printed in Hong Kong
Designed by Depke Design

04 03 02 01 00
10 9 8 7 6 5 4 3 2 1

Library of Congress Cataloging-in-Publication Data
Ansary, Mir Tamim.
    Subarctic Indians / Mir Tamim Ansary.
       p. cm. - (Native Americans)
    Includes bibliographical references and index.
    Summary: An introduction to the history, dwellings, artwork,
religious beliefs, clothing, and food of the various Native American
tribes of the Subarctic, the large area south of the Arctic.
    ISBN 1-57572-926-1 (library binding)
    1. Athabascan Indians Juvenile literature. 2. Algonquian Indians
Juvenile literature. 3. Indians of North America-Canada Juvenile
literature. 4. Indians of North America-Alaska Juvenile literature.
[1. Indians of North America-Canada. 2. Indians of North America-
Alaska.] I. Title. II. Series: Ansary, Mir Tamim. Native Americans.
E99.A86A57 2000
979.8'004972-dc21
                                                          99-34899
                                                          CIP

Acknowledgments
The author and publishers are grateful to the following for permission to reproduce copyright material:
Cover: HBCA/PAM
AP/Wide World Photos, p. 30 top; B&C Alexander/Photo Researchers, Inc., p. 17; Ben Klaffek, p. 13; The Bridgeman Art
Library, p. 11; Dr. E.R. Degginger, pp. 5, 8, 24; The Granger Collection, pp. 14, 30 bottom; Calvin Goggleye, p. 29;
HBCA/PAM, pp. 7, 18, 19, 23, 25, 27; Milwaukee Public Museum of Milwaukee County, p. 12; North Wind Pictures,
pp. 10, 16, 22, 26; Maria Stenzel/National Geographic Image Collection, pp. 9, 28; Marilyn Angel Wynn, pp. 15, 20, 21.

Every effort has been made to contact copyright holders of any material reproduced in this book. Any omissions will be
rectified in subsequent printings if notice is given to the publisher.

Our special thanks to Lana Grant, Native American MLS, for her
help in the preparation of this book.

Note to the Reader Some words are shown in bold, **like this.** You can find
out what they mean by looking in the glossary.

Contents

The Subarctic Region

The Subarctic is a large area of land south of the Arctic. It stretches from Alaska to north east Canada, covering two million square miles (5 million square kilometers. This land is cold and mostly flat. The southern part is covered with woods. Farther north, the temperature drops and the woods thin out.

In some areas of the Subarctic, a layer of soil below the ground is always frozen. But snow melts in late spring. Then **bogs** and lakes appear. Blackflies and mosquitoes swarm over these waters. Millions of birds nest among the bogs. The woods are thick with woodland **caribou**, beavers, and other animals.

Bering Sea

ARCTIC OCEAN

Beaufort Sea

Baffin Bay

SUBARCTIC

Labrador Sea

PACIFIC OCEAN

NORTH AMERICA

ATLANTIC OCEAN

N

Areas where Subarctic Indians live

500 miles
800 kilometers

People of the Subarctic

The Indians of the western Subarctic came from Siberia, a part of Asia. They crossed into North America only five or six thousand years ago. They divided into many tribes, such as the Chippewyans, the Yellowknife, the Slavey, and others. Their languages are still related. All belong to the *Athabaskan* language group.

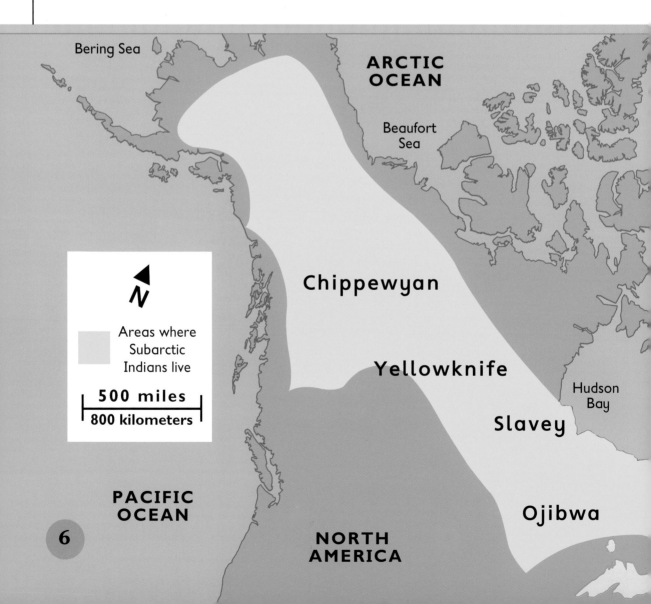

Bering Sea

ARCTIC OCEAN

Beaufort Sea

N

Areas where Subarctic Indians live

500 miles
800 kilometers

Chippewyan

Yellowknife

Hudson Bay

Slavey

Ojibwa

PACIFIC OCEAN

NORTH AMERICA

6

The Indians around the south and east coasts of Hudson Bay have a different history. They speak *Algonquin* languages. Their **ancestors** came from Siberia, too, but much earlier. They crossed into North America at least 10,000 years ago. The Cree, Ojibwa, Naskapi, and Montaignis are some of these Algonquin-speaking tribes.

Labrador Sea

This family is Cree, an important tribe of the southern Subarctic region.

Naskapi

Montaignis

ATLANTIC OCEAN

Cree

Food

Most Subarctic tribes gathered wild plants, berries, and nuts for food. Many Subarctic people also lived by hunting and fishing. Some adults ate up to four pounds of meat a day. They liked fatty meats, which helped keep them warm. Beavers, for example, were a main food for the Cree.

Beavers were important to the Cree and others for their fur as well as their meat.

The more slowly meat was smoked, the longer it would last.

Caribou, moose, geese, and bears were hunted, too.
They were hunted with **traps** and spears and knives
and clubs. Meat was often smoked for days over a
green wood fire. Meat cooked in this way would
stay edible for months. The Kutchin smoked salmon
and other fish in this same way.

Shelter in a Cold Land

Western tribes sometimes made log or plank cabins. They were **nomads**, but they traveled the same **routes** every year. So they used the same cabins every year. They often left food and seeds behind when they moved on. When they came back again, they had something they could eat right away.

Cabins like this were often built in open areas next to lakes.

Sometimes two wigwams like this were joined together and a fire was made at each end.

The eastern tribes lived in wigwams. A wigwam was a tentlike house. The walls were made of animal skins or strips of bark. These were wrapped around a cone-shaped frame of poles. A winter wigwam had double walls, with moss in between to act as insulation. Inside, a pole was tied across the open space. Shoes, clothes, and food could be hung here to dry.

Dressing for Warmth

The Subarctic Indians made their clothes out of animal skins. Women worked the skins into a leather as soft as cloth. A **caribou hide,** for example, was boiled, scraped, pounded, rubbed with caribou brains, and worked by hand. Then it was smoked. Smoked leather kept mosquitoes and flies away.

This deer hide will be stretched, soaked, scraped, and worked by hand until it softens into leather.

These beaded moccasins are also leggings.

Men wore leather shirts. Women wore leather
dresses. Most people wore leggings made of leather.
Soft shoes called moccasins were often sewn right
to the leggings. In winter, people wore snowshoes
decorated with colored rabbit fur. The fur made
them easy to find in the snow.

Art in Daily Life

Though life was hard in the Subarctic, people found time for art. During the cold winter months, they decorated many of the goods they used in everyday life. They wove beautiful bags, boxes, belts, and carrying straps. They made these items out of bark, strips of leather, porcupine quills, and colored shells.

The Cree began using flowerlike patterns in their art after meeting and trading with White people.

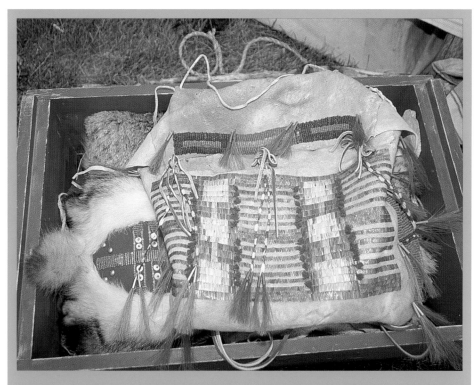

The patterns on this bag are made of dyed porcupine quills woven together.

Clothes were a form of art as well. Dogrib women decorated their leather dresses with red and white porcupine quills. The Naskapi painted designs on their clothes with red and yellow dyes. The Cree made fur coats with a picture of the animal painted inside the coat. Flower designs were common among the Ojibwa. These designs were thought to represent recipes from nature.

Family Bands

People lived in small, scattered family bands, or groups, depending on the season. In the summer, several such bands came together. They camped next to a lake or a river for a few weeks. They shared news, told stories, played drums, and had fun. A marriage or two might come out of such a gathering.

Summer gatherings were times of fun for the Indian people of the Subarctic.

A Cree trapper takes a fish from the net he set under the ice of a frozen lake.

As summer ended, the gatherings broke up. Each band moved away on its own to hunt and fish or harvest wild rice. Big animals were hunted for their meat in the fall when they were fattest. Animals with fur were trapped in early winter. That's when they had the thickest coats.

Deep Winter

Subarctic winters are cold and dark and the nights are very long. In the middle of winter, no one went out much. Families spent these months making the goods they needed and telling important tribal stories. They worked animal **hides** into leather. Women wove bags and decorated clothes.

Storytelling helped pass the long winter nights, when families had to stay indoors.

18

Scary stories helped to keep children from wandering away into the woods alone.

Elders told stories to pass the time and to teach. Some of the stories were scary. The Cree, for example, told tales about the *windigo*. This monster started out as a human. But it got separated from other people. Living alone in the forest turned it into a horrible people-eating giant.

Dreams and Spirits

Hunters feared and respected the animals they killed. They honored these animals' spirits. The Cree, for example, returned a beaver's bones to the river. Many people wore necklaces of animal parts such as bear claws. They hoped to gain the animal's powers with such necklaces.

A necklace with animal teeth was thought to give its owner certain powers.

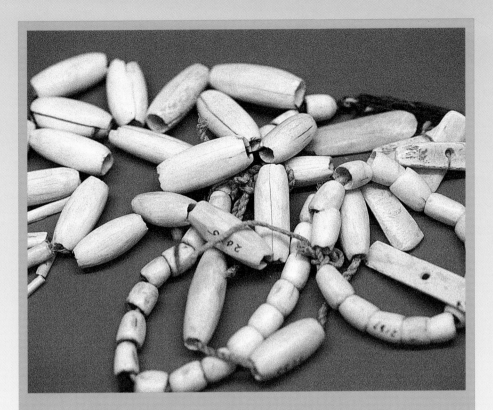

Bone beads like these could help a shaman search for answers to important questions.

Some men and women became shamans. A shaman, it was thought, could cure illness and give powerful advice. Shamans looked for answers in their dreams. Naskapi shamans used animal bones, too. They heated a bone till cracks appeared. They "read" the cracks to help with healing and in giving advice.

Europeans Arrive

By the late 1500s, Europeans were exploring the Subarctic. In 1670, the English set up the Hudson's Bay Company to trade with Indians. This company built **trading posts** all across the Subarctic. The English traded beads, cloth, and other goods for fur and Indian artwork.

Native Americans were glad to trade fur for beads, which they used to decorate clothes and other goods.

A Slavey woman in British Columbia makes moccasins for sale.

Indian women began making goods for sale instead of for their own use. They made goods that Europeans liked. To meet the Europeans' need for many furs, Indians started trapping more animals than they needed themselves. Soon, there were fewer animals, and some Indians began to starve.

War and Disease

Wars broke out in the Subarctic for the first time. The Chippewyans fought to keep the Yellowknives away from the Europeans. They wanted to be the only Indians to trade with the Europeans. The Cree got guns and drove other tribes north. The Slaveys started forest fires to make White **trappers** and traders go away.

As White people pushed into the Subarctic, fighting and other problems spread among the Indians.

This peaceful picture shows a Cree village before the Europeans came to the region.

But the Europeans would not go away. Diseases they brought to the Subarctic killed many Indians. **Smallpox** killed most of the Chippewyans in the 1780s. In 1917, the flu killed many more Indians. War and disease totally wiped out an eastern tribe called the Beothuk.

The 20th Century

In the late 1920s, hard times hit the United States and Canada. Many people lost their jobs, homes, and farms. Many White people moved to the Subarctic to make money from trapping. But White **trappers** almost wiped out the fur-bearing animals of this region.

White trappers who needed money saw the Subarctic as a land of opportunity.

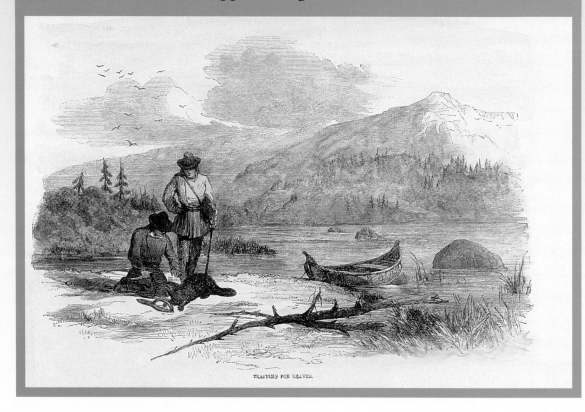

TRAPPING FOR BEAVER.

Traps like this kill or cripple any animal that steps into them.

The White trappers used steel traps that killed all kinds of animals, not just the ones with fur. They trapped pregnant beavers before they could give birth. So fewer beavers were born each year. Luckily, by 1940, the price of fur had dropped. Most of the White trappers went away then.

The Subarctic Today

Today, many Indians of the Subarctic work in mining and other industries. Many, however, still hunt and trap. Their careful methods have allowed the animals to come back. Beavers, otters, and other animals are plentiful again. No animal trapped for its fur is now **endangered** in the Subarctic.

The Native Americans of the Subarctic now use modern tools, such as this power boat.

*The Native Americans of the Leech Lake Reservation sell
wild rice to make money.*

At the southern edge of the region, the Chippewa
and Ojibwa have made a business out of gathering
wild rice. Minnesota's Leech Lake **Reservation** has
55 wild rice fields—the most in North America.
Trade of this kind now connects the Indians of the
Subarctic to the whole world.

Famous Subarctic Indians

Buffy Sainte-Marie (Cree, 1942–) was born on the Piapot Indian **Reservation** in Canada. She became one of the most famous folk singers of the 1960s with hits like "Universal Soldier" and "Where Have the Buffalo Gone?" In the 1970s, she often sang on the children's TV show Sesame Street.

Jim Thorpe (Sac/Fox, 1888–1953) was a champion at track, swimming, lacrosse, and hockey. He won two gold medals at the 1912 Olympic Games. Later he played both professional baseball and professional football. Many call Thorpe the greatest athlete of the 20th century.

Wub-e-ke-niew (Ojibwa, 1928–) helped found the American Indian Movement in 1965. This group fights for the rights of Native Americans. In 1995, Wub-e-ke-niew published the book *We Have the Right to Exist.* It is the only book about Ojibwa teachings from an Ojibwa point of view.

Glossary

ancestor person who comes earlier in a family, especially before a grandparent

bog area of wet, soft ground

caribou largest member of the deer family

craft something made skillfully by hand; or the skill of making such objects

endangered in danger of becoming extinct

hide skin of a large animal, usually with the fur still attached

language group group of languages that are related

nomad person who moves from place to place and has no permanent home

reservation area of land set aside for Native Americans

route path that is used often to get from place to place

smallpox deadly disease that causes a high fever and sores on the skin, now very uncommon

trading post store where outsiders to an area live and trade with the local people

trapper person who catches animals

More Books to Read

Lund, Bill. *The Ojibwa Indians.* Danbury, Conn.: Children's Press, 1997.

Regguinti, Gordon. *The Sacred Harvest: Ojibway Wild Rice Gathering.* Minneapolis Minn.: Lerner Publishing Group, 1992.

Farrell, Edward. *Young Jim Thorpe: All-American Athlete.* Mahwah, N.J.: Troll Communications, 1997.

Index

DATE DUE

11/24/04			

#47-0108 Peel Off Pressure Sensitive